American Flamingo

CRAB ORCHARD SERIES IN POETRY

Open Competition Award

American Flamingo

∿ GREG PAPE

Crab Orchard Review

& Southern Illinois University Press

CARBONDALE

Printed in the United States of America

08   07   06   05   4   3   2   1

The Crab Orchard Series in Poetry is a joint publishing venture of Southern
Illinois University Press and *Crab Orchard Review*. This series has been
made possible by the generous support of the Office of the President of
Southern Illinois University and the Office of the Vice Chancellor for
Academic Affairs and Provost at Southern Illinois University Carbondale.

Crab Orchard Series in Poetry Editor: Jon Tribble
Open Competition Award Judge for 2004: Richard Cecil

Library of Congress Cataloging-in-Publication Data

Pape, Greg, [date]
 American flamingo / Greg Pape.
   p. cm. — (Crab Orchard series in poetry)
I. Title. II. Series: Crab Orchard award series in poetry
PS3566.A614A83 2005
811'.54—dc22
ISBN 0-8093-2621-3 (cloth : alk. paper)
ISBN 0-8093-2622-1 (alk. paper)   2004022124

Printed on recycled paper. ♻

The paper used in this publication meets the minimum requirements
of American National Standard for Information Sciences—Permanence
of Paper for Printed Library Materials, ANSI Z39.48-1992. ∞

For my sons, Coleman and Clay

Contents

Acknowledgments

My thanks to the editors of the following publications in which these poems appeared (sometimes in slightly different form):

The Atlantic Monthly — "American Flamingo" and "Fog" (Part 10 of "Album")
Big Sky Journal — "Bitterroot Car-Body Riprap"
Black Warrior Review — "Whatever Happened to J.C.?" and "Evening News" (Parts 2 and 3 of "Elegy for the Duke of Earl")
Cutbank — "The Ani" and "Remember the Moose"
DoubleTake — "Zahkia"
Gulf Coast — "Practice" and "The Rose"
Headwaters: Montana Writers on Water and Wilderness — "Bitterroot Car-Body Riprap"
Louisville Review — "Trying to Judge" (Part 3 of "Album")
Luna — "Keet Seel," "Morphine," and "Unfinished Story"
Mid-American Review — "Bitterroot Car-Body Riprap" and "The Flying Red Horse" (Part 1 of "Elegy for the Duke of Earl")
Ploughshares — "Snow Storm"
Poetry — "Image on a Sandstone Disc"
Quarterly West — "Kindness of Strangers," "As Sparks Fly Upward," and "Fireworks"
Shenandoah — "First Hour" and "Indian River"
Talking River Review — "Green," "For Clay" (Part 1 of "Album"), and "Animals"
Natural Bridge — "We Are"

Some of these poems appeared in a limited edition chapbook entitled *Small Pleasures*, Lagniappe Press, 1994.

Special thanks to Chris Dombrowski, Nana Lampton, Malena Mörling, Sena Jeter Naslund, Tammy Ramsey, and Frank X Walker for friendship, encouragement, and support. Thanks to Richard Cecil. Thanks also to my family: Irene, Larry, and Kay Pape, Dr. Arthur J. Prange Jr., Sally Bowen Prange, Kevin Woodman, Marnie, Coleman, and Clay.

American Flamingo

Image on a Sandstone Disc

Moundville, Alabama

Snakes conjured up
   through the ripples,
      convolutions, and sleek passages

of the new brain
   from the old.
      Snakes

with fangs,
   forked tongues, rattles
      and horns.

Two snakes
   tied together in two knots,
      heads to tails.

In the circle they make
   an open eye
      in an open palm.

The meaning is lost,
   they say. Read this image,
      symbol of an old human community,

know you are guessing,
   reading with the wrong eyes.
      Read it anyway.

The snakes are power,
   the knots, restraint,
      an image of fear

and force,
    not overcome, but contained —
        a fire

they danced around,
    and sang.
        The eye in the palm

is the gift of vision.
    It says
        we all belong.

See the circle
    and the fire, hear
        the drum

and the turning of an old human song,
    close and far away
        like a river,

its rocky hum and weedy sway,
    a river we stand in
        and is gone.

One

First Hour

Bitterroot Mountains, Montana

Just before dawn a heavy snow is falling
that's been falling for hours. No wind.
No sound. I walk so slowly even the coyote
trotting down through lodgepoles along the creek
doesn't see me until she is so close she hits
the wall of my scent, turns in a splash of snow
and doubles her pace back up the slope.
The snow lightens then stops.
I could follow her if I wanted to, the tracks
are so clear. No telling where she might
take me. I look up the trail, an opening
of faint blue light, pines black against the snow,
until the trail turns from sight. My steps slow,
my eyes move side to side, up the slope
and down. I stop to study two sets of tracks,
deer heading up slope, and a spider half
the diameter of a dime steps up from the dark
pit of a hoof print. Its spidery steps are tentative,
weakened as though stunned by the snow.
I lean down over the spider, who stops
at the approach of such a massive shadow,
then steps back into the pit of the deer track.
I go slowly up the trail, step over one
then another until it seems all the spiders
making a home in the pines have been knocked
down. A gusty blue note blows across the snow.
In the fullness of the first hour, grateful
for this life, I go on up the mountain—
blue shadows at the verge of sight.

The River Comes Closer

An owl calls across the river.

Another answers farther downstream.

Stars glitter through the branches of pines
and on the back of the river.

He sits still, leaning against a tree.
The river comes a little closer.

Deer come closer.

He hears the riffle upstream
and the one down. Water eddies
and runs susurrous in his mind.

Looking up into the sweeping current of starlight,
fish idle and hold against the flow.

Now, just above his head, a third owl calls—
six blue notes like circles widening on the surface of a pool,
picked up and repeated across the river,
then down away.

The sound goes around, an echo, an eddy
in the dark before dawn.

He listens, slips his hand into the cold river,
turns it over, palm up, to cup the water
to hold stars.

Remember the Moose

She must have come down from high mountain meadows
    where bear-grass blooms
had dried and fallen, paintbrush put away its colors, and mud-wallows
    begun to freeze
and stay frozen past noon, down along the creek through aspen,
    alder, and willow thickets
to high grass along a road leading to town.

Why she kept on coming you can only guess. Rich green smell
    of cemetery grass,
muted bellow of a distant bull, old path imprinted in her genes,
    deep doubts,
simple curiosity? Maybe she was lost, or came as a reminder
    of something lost.
A moose grazing among the graves on Sunset Hill is an image
    one might hold
for years, turning it over and over, working it into a story or
    finding it,
strangely lit, inverted in a dream.

Remember the moose outside the tent in Idaho, the moonlight
    and mosquitos,
how she looked like a boulder in the creek until she lifted
    her great head
from the water, big worldly angel, and turned to look at you
    with ropes
of weeds hanging from her mouth.

By day she strolled among the park's swing sets and jungle gyms,
    stopping to sniff
the dull shine of a slide or stopping, high as a house, in some child's
    eye.

Parents, sensing danger, tried to shoo her away, but she followed
    her own calling.
Nearly blind after the sun went down, street lights and house lights
    surrounded her—
a confusion of moons. She must have picked one to lead her on.
    They found her
on the Newsome's front porch, snout pressed against the wall,
    back legs splayed.
Terrified, someone said, as neighbors gathered to watch the wildlife
    officials load their darts
and end her urban visit in a sudden blur of drugs.

Think of Golden Gate Park half a life ago, a day of dancing
    and chanting,
thousands of hairy kids, men, women, dogs with beads and
    dirty bandanas,
a fog of breath and marijuana pulsing around black banks
    of speakers
blasting the twilight with drumbeat and guitar shrieks.
    Someone smiling
hands you a hit of something. You walk off across a baseball
    diamond
toward some tree or siren or patch of grass looking for your
    country.
A shock-eyed man marches barefoot mouthing a manic recitation
    like a fuse burning.
You walk and walk into dark and stare at the moon until it
    comes down
and covers your face with its bowl of white light.

After the drugs took hold the drugs wore off. They loaded
    her on a truck,
gently as they could, drove her out of town on dirt roads,
    lifted her down
into high grass, waited to see her waken.

Think of leaving and coming back. Think what you have nurtured
   and betrayed.
Think of the towns and cities you changed with your absence.
   Think of the country.
Remember the moose turning away, lowering her head into the water,
   leaving you
the afterimage — unspoken words, weeds hanging from your mouth.
   Remember waking
in a colder place, glad to breathe and see your breath.

Snow Storm

Washington, D.C.

The taxi driver from Sierra Leone, who missed his home,
but doubted he would ever go back, maneuvered
the cab on its bald tires in the snow and slush
like a fish through the sparse traffic
from Washington Circle to the Museum of Natural History.
The people in charge of my country, he said,
are killers.

He left me standing on the curb in the snow,
thinking: he can't go home, this man from the Lion
Mountains driving away in a taxi on the icy streets of D.C.

And though I wanted to see the great up-thrust tusks
of the mammoth, and feel something
of the tidal pull of time outside the small hotel room
where I'd been working — reading and commenting
on other people's writing, one woman whose name
stayed with me, Memuna Sillah, from Sierra Leone,
who wrote gracefully about her arranged marriage
that involved a whole village, her immigration
to New York, her subsequent divorce — though I wanted
to rest my eyes on fossils and bones, gaze
at dioramas, ease away awhile from the human,

a security guard and a snow-plow driver
welcomed me into the museum's vestibule
with the news the museum was closed:
"Whole government's shut down," one said.
And the other joked, "They knew you was comin', man."

Snow piled on the shoulders of Rochambeau,
on the blowing cape sculpted in bronze of the woman,
I thought, Memuna Sillah, standing with her left hand

full of banners, and in her right hand a sword, who
seemed to be guarding the guardian eagle of the republic,
which might as well have been a lion. And snow
piled on the wide green leaves of a magnolia
protected, between buildings, from the wind.
Hours it seemed, her name, Memuna Sillah,
accompanied me on my walk through the storm.

I stopped to watch the Washington Monument,
dressed in scaffolding, its spire fading
and sharpening, in sheets of blowing snow.
Closer, on the curb, under a big mound
of trash bags, plastic bottles tied with string,
overlaid with cardboard, carpet scraps, and snow —

under all this, waiting out the storm, I supposed
the dream of freedom persisted. And the snow
blowing and drifting, holding this hostage
face down on the curb, settled softly, all around,
against stone walls.

Fishing Party, 1890s

(Photograph by Myrta Wright Stevens)

Of the party only one
appears to be having fun.
She is nearly knee deep
in the cold water of Lolo Creek,
her long skirt hiked up. Is she
smiling goodbye to the nineteenth century

or to her fly? Except for one of the dogs
who looks at the camera, alert, eager,
ready to run, she is the only one smiling,
the only one fishing.
The other women, flowered hats, long dresses
and gloves, look uncomfortable holding rods

as though this were someone else's idea.
They wait their turn while the one smiling is either
enjoying the fishing or the comic absurdity
of this posed photograph she will be
a part of longer than she will live. The men
look stern. The two with rifles seem

to be armed guards. The older man
with a rod, standing behind the woman
fishing, gazes critically downstream
as though he knew where the creek
and the future were headed and didn't approve. The dogs,
of course, look just like twenty-first-century dogs.

The Ani

October, November, December, I've forgotten
the month, but I remember the moment
I first saw the Ani

perched on the limb of a young tree
planted in the divider strip of a parking lot
in South Florida, North Miami, Bay Vista,

where they used to dump toxic waste
in the mangroves, then paved it over
and built a university. I worked there

two years. The limb was so slight
and the Ani so heavy it bobbed
up and down in the breeze.

Clouds loomed above the sea.
Tar-black and shining in the sun,
its big grotesque beak

in profile, it looked straight at me
with one eye glinting like a black pearl.
I am the Lord God of this exact place
it said. Who are you?

Practice

Miami Beach, Florida

Lux et Veritas. Light and Truth. A good motto,
along with *Levavi Oculos,* raise your eyes, look up,
lift your spirit.

There is a photo of my mother, a young woman
lying on a beach towel looking up
with such a radiant loving smile, just to recall it
I am fortified.

Take this, sweetheart, she seems to say,
and put it right in there with the big abstractions.

We do battle with truth and each other.
Something, *it,* escapes us. We love it,
but we don't get it. At least not often enough.

So it goes, we say, and then it doesn't.

Hungry, thinking these thoughts, I stop
at a fast food place on Collins.

I take my burger, fries and Coke, on a red tray,
to a table near the window to sit in the light
and watch.

The steady traffic, the changing light, the old
beachfront hotels and apartment buildings,
some occupied, some abandoned.

Rooms where the honeymooners honeymooned,
where runaways and the homeless hide.

My mother told me, this used to be known,
back in the forties, as Chicago Beach
because of all the people from Chicago
who vacationed here in the winter.

I sip my Coke and imagine card games
on beach towels, baby oil on sunburned backs.

Levavi Oculos. I look up
to see the reassuring blue of the sky,
and someone flings a rope
from the top of the building.

 A man in green fatigues,
a pump gun strapped over his shoulder,
rappels down the face of the building,
stops abruptly next to a closed window,
unshoulders the gun, pumps a shell
into the chamber, smashes the glass
with the gun-butt, turns the barrel
into the dark room and fires and fires again.

Someone is dead or about to die, I think,
but before an image of that room
can form in the vacuum after the blasts,
the routine way he reshoulders the gun
tells me this is practice. I am watching
the S.W.A.T. team practice.

He drops down the rope in no great hurry.

I look up in the light.

Another man in green fatigues
steps off the roof, rappels down the rope,
fires two blasts into the room and so on.

Lux et Veritas   Levavi Oculos

Bitterroot Car-Body Riprap

When we float the Bitterroot on the home stretch
    I love between Stevensville bridge
and Florence bridge we look forward to these wrecked
    banks, this grave calm and slow current
where big trout rise like lively ghosts.
But whose idea was this to line the banks
    of the pristine river with the damaged
shells of our passage through the tranquilized
    fifties, the cast-off rusting hulks of our
nearsighted hallucinatory transport to and from
    the hairy marches of the sixties?
Who first conceived an end to oxbowing
    by cabling car-bodies against the pure force
of a wandering stream? Was it the pragmatism of lists
    and ledgers penciled and memoed and droned
on the phone until the merely expedient fluoresced
    into the surreal? Or was it the product
of a single vision, some warden who for years
    stared at the wreck of a Studebaker
wedged between rocks, and forming a small eddy,
    in the same spot it had come to rest
after the poor intoxicated driver had broken
    through the guardrail and left the road for good?
Did the idea strike like a trout in slow water —
    put these wrecks to some good use?
One form of erosion against another? This scene
    oscillates between the accidentally sacramental
and the sinister, between a mass baptism and a drowning.
Look at them with their noses in the river,
    these sad clownish battered metal purely
American products, their broken eyes aswim,
    their fixed grins full of gravel.

Album

Bitterroot Valley, Montana

1.

Call it beautiful timing,
    the way Kristin, the doctor,
Lifted, with the backs of two fingers,
    the umbilical cord
Away from your throat
    and slipped it over your head as
You entered the communal air
    of our lives.

Bless her skilled
    hands and bet
On us to keep
    the blessings coming.
We, your mother and I,
    are wild about you.
Even guessing
    what we will all go through —
Nights without sleep,
    nervous breakdown, failures of

Patience, and so on — we wouldn't trade
    this life with you for
Anything. Though we all dissolve, eventually,
    into the earth of our names,
Pace yourself, and believe
    that loving part of us is with you
Even when you
    are most alone.

2.

I walk along a trail toward the Bitterroot River
with fourteen-month-old Clay in the backpack
singing a trail song in my ear, a breathy song
among sharper sounds of meadowlarks,
red-wing blackbirds, distant geese above
the trees. *Shee hah Shee hah Shee Shee*
hah, he sings over and over, soft sounds
in rhythm with my steps, and then it changes,
as we approach the banks, to liquid labials
untranscribable as the speech of the river.

Coleman, five, and Clay, three, are throwing rocks
from the front porch across the small ditch.
The dog is lying in the grass near the apple tree,
just out of range. The boys have gathered a box
full of rocks, ammo for the siege. They duck
behind the porch rail and come up firing.

I am watering the garden down the slope below
the dog, trying to judge whether or not she is
in danger, whether or not I should stop the barrage.
We've all been cooped up in the house for hours —
wind, thunder, lightning, but only a few drops
of rain. Now the sun is out. The dog is old.
It hurts her to walk. She looks at these annoying
puppies who have stroked her tenderly, who have
displaced her in the order of the pack. Just as she
decides to move, and I decide to holler, a rock
hits her in the tail.

The soldiers are triumphant and guilty.
I head up the slope to the porch. "What do you
think you're doing?" Coleman tries to explain.
"It was by mistakely. We were playing war.
It was the first time. No, it was the second time."
"When was the first time?" I ask. Coleman relaxes.
He has read the limit of my anger. He grins,
makes himself small, puts on a fierce face, crooks
his fingers into claws. Clay watches wide-eyed.
"The first time," he answers, "was way back
when me and Clay were inside Mom."

4.

First it's thin as a trout bone
poking through pines in white fire
on the ridge above Gold Creek.
Ghost horn of God's white rhino
turned scimitar of blind light.
First day of February,
crescent moon rising over
the Sapphire Mountains, drifting
south, followed by a pink glow
washing up, raying, dawning.

My son wakes, comes down the stairs.
Dad, you know what we forgot?
What did we forget? Something.

The moon dissolves in daylight.

5.

My seven-year-old son draws a series
of strong hearts. He puts a face on the heart,
eyes that look straight out at the world,

a single line for eyebrows and nose,
a confident smiling or smirking mouth
unafraid to speak, poised and ready there

in the center of the face of the heart.
Where ears should be, arms curl out
flexing biceps round as baseballs.

The long legs are ready to run or dance
or jump the hurdles placed before the heart.
These drawings speak clearly of the spirit

in him. Father, they say, don't scold me.
I am proud. There is so little difference now
between the outer and inner life.

Father, they say, guard me
with your love, and I will go on
being strong when you are gone.

6.

Down at the edge of the coulee,
deer lie waiting for the sun
to warm them into motion.

Only their darker ears, listening,
show like mullein among
the knapweed. Faint waves

of a scent or sound turn a head
to profile in morning light.
One doe muscles up, stretches

and begins that rhythm of drift
and poise we share in the morning,
buff bodies hungering
over the buff skin of the hills.

7.

The day begins with *Bolero*. *Bolero* in unbalanced
stereo coming down through the joists of the floor
above. It is still dark. Deer are feeding
on the green tomatoes a few feet from the window,
their erect ears darker against the dark, listening.
I know the music, but the name has not yet
come to me, still adrift between the day and last
vivid dream in which she came to me, my good
friend, my wife's friend, undressed and curled
against me, moved her smooth thigh against
my thigh, kissed my ear and rolled gracefully up
and over me and slipped away looking back
tenderly over her bare shoulder saying no, no.

An elephant rocks and slowly rises from a mud-
wallow bristling with iridescent flies. There is
a droning, a ground wave of distant dry savanna,
a sound not yet music. It is a labor to stand
and assume the dignity the day requires. The high-
stepping trumpets turn and begin to march.
The sunflowers, old monks in rags, bow to the ground
their seed-heavy heads. They will not stare again
at the sun. No. They weep their seeds into the ground.
They do not listen to the building strains of *Bolero*
that move my sons to gallop like riderless horses
over the pastures of morning.

8.

The wild cat hunched on the woodpile can't remember
where it used to live, can't decide where to go,

but the storm that's on its way has already arrived
in the electromagnetic spectrum of its small brain.

The old dog limps to the edge of the yard to bark
at the deer, who raise their heads but don't bother to run.

Yarded up since Christmas Eve, they seem to be saving
their strength for the next storm.

Balanced on the porch railing, bearing a dead geranium,
a red clay pot, like a small fire in the gloom

or a beautiful face, has ridden out the winter
in all its fierceness so far.

At the insistence of the wind, a few more rotted cottonwoods
have fallen and lie like the wounded in shock,

feeling no pain, past caring. Left alone,
they will be a good long time dying.

Pine seedlings planted by birds push up through the snow.
Those birds, the raucous Clark's nutcrackers

haven't returned from their winter wanderings.
They are busy somewhere south

harvesting and planting, filling their beaks
and pouches under their tongues with pine nuts.

It's a good thing they never find again
most of what they've hidden in the ground.

9. LATE MARCH

After dinner, just before sunset
the boys go out to shoot hoops.

Something happens. The younger one,
six, comes back in to an empty room,

throws himself into a chair and cries.
I come in and ask what's wrong.

He pulls his red shirt up over his face
and through his sobbing says,

I don't want to tell you. It's okay,
I say, you don't have to tell me.

I pat him gently on the head
and then his back. It's so hard,

he sobs, it's so hard to play hoops
with my brother. I pick him up

and set him on my lap and try
to comfort him. It's so hard, he says,

it's too cold. I can't play in my coat
and my pack boots. The ball hurts

my hand. There there, I say.
When is it going to be summer?

I don't like school all the time.
I don't like scouts. I want it to be warm.
When can I stay home and be warm?

10.

My son has built a tent-cabin
in the front room and invited in the dog.

He has constructed an imaginary machine,
with an invisible lever, for catching the fog.

Fallen clouds drifting through the valley
along the river-bottom, up and over the lines

and folds and contours of the hills, coulees
and benches, combed by cottonwoods and pines,

breaking softly against the windows
like thought or breath, then passing on,

flowing, opaque body of air, and we are both
caught up in this elemental conversation

of house and fog. The fog got in the house,
he says. I am catching it with this.

Idling

Sitting on the seawall at the southern end
of Key Biscayne, with a line in the water,
he moves his gaze like a sable brush
from the breast of an idling gull
to the weathered gray wood of the houses
on stilts out in the bay,
from the long swaying branches of Australian pines
that will blow away in the next hurricane
to the endangered coral rocks and white sands
that turn the blue of the sky to the blue-green of the bay,
from the spiny rock lobsters (for the taking of which
may result in fines and imprisonment)
to the horse conchs (also illegal),
from the long white expensive boats
to the rainbowed fabric of sails,
from the flashing towers and banked glass facades
of vacant condominiums to the stuttering path
of a police helicopter, unsure if he's guilty
or innocent, feeling the pull of local currents
and solunar tides, he holds his line,
lightly, between forefinger and thumb,
not to keep from falling, believing falling
is half the secret, but to feel the tug
of the other half when it comes for its prey.

Reading

He had been reading the novel at night
before sleep for two weeks.
Not every night, but nearly every night.
It was a pleasure more than an escape,
though part of the pleasure was the sense
of release, of letting go his own concerns
or loosening his hold on things
to hold the story, or part of the story
of someone else's life for awhile.
It was a good story. He liked those people.
All of them. Even the one who caused
the others so much trouble and pain.
The young man, call him Dell, who died, did so
only in the imagined lives of the others
who loved him. As he read,
Dell came to life again, and he began
to understand why the others loved Dell,
who died again and went on living in the others
in the most unexpected ways. It was an odd kind
of pleasure he took in Dell's death,
without trouble or pain. He didn't want
the book to end. So he read slowly,
but finally it was too good to stop
and he read, feeling welling up,
to the end. Then he read the beginning again.

The Oldest Thing

Sonora Desert, Arizona

A one-inch-diameter hole
in the plexiglass, and behind that
a dark rock, darkened more
by the oils from countless human fingers.
I put my finger in the hole
and touch the Allende meteorite,
adding my oils to the others,
as I read the sign, ". . . at 4.6 billion
years, this is the oldest thing
you will ever touch. It was formed
before the Earth, and parts of it
may be older than the Sun."
Reverently I stand in the semi-dark
beneath the Sonora Desert
among other visitors trying to imagine.
I note the little round grains
on the meteorite, "chondrules,
bits of primordial matter
that were once molten droplets
formed from our solar system's
original dust and gas."
I bow to the chondrule
and I am proud of the oil,
my part in the darkening.
Long may the human fingers
darken the meteorite. Someone says,
"Janet, Janet, touch this!"
It's the oldest thing. But Janet
is more interested in a piece of the moon,
a basaltic rock from Crater Camelot
near the Taurus Mountains
at the southeast edge of Mare Serenitatis.

A Pair of Mallards

A winter sun lights a pair of mallards
standing on the ice at the edge of smooth water.

Another pair mirrored beneath them
in the floating world among mountains, five
bare cottonwoods and a single pine.

Orange legs, iridescent green head of the drake,
the brightest things in the landscape today.

Now they are preening breast feathers,
stretching their legs, perfectly at home,
I think as I look up from my notes
to find them gone.

Small waves radiate over the surface.
They must have stepped from the ice ledge
and used the water to take off. Gone
now into the winter sky and water mirror

those orange legs standing over the image
of orange legs and the drake's green head,
the many overlaid feathers accepting the light
that keeps on arriving, moving the light,

moving the gaze away from the hen
whose mottled feathers
wear the muted colors of the land.

Animals

Bird song, sunshine, hissing and blowing
    traffic sounds of highway 61
just north of Red Wing, Minnesota.
    I sit up in the treetops at Tower View
on a small balcony above the back porch
    taking note. Leaves of grape ivy
cling to the bricks and wave in a slight breeze.
    This is going to take patience.
Four lightning rods, one leaning west,
    prick the sky along the roof-ridge.
A pigeon paces like a worried mother
    on the big chimney. Robin, finch,
sparrow, and swallow show themselves
    among the leaves.

When I began to wake up and love my life,
    for a long time most of the animals
I noticed were dead: torn rag of a dog
    on the road, bloated deer like a turned-
over table for the ants, leathery carcass
    of cat, and all those nameless
butterflies and birds one could pick
    from the teeth of Plymouths and Fords.
Even in the moonlight of a Mexican beach
    beside a thatch-roofed café strolling
out arm in arm with my lover
    after dinner, the only animals
to be found were a dozen filleted iguanas,
    their limp tails draped
over the rim of a fifty-gallon drum.
    Love and death rubbed together
like money in a wallet. Even my wallet,
    I remember now, was skin from a water buffalo.

Then the names of things became more important.
    With a name one could hold on,
not lose so much. Anger, fear, love
    can twist the tongue silly or clamp it tight.
But say a name and it rings. What
    should I call my dream animal,
my bear, my otter, my carp, my lover
    of clear streams and muddy lakes? You?

Yesterday walking with my friend Hanzlicek,
    we came upon a big mossy-backed
snapping turtle digging a hole for her eggs
    next to a foot bridge over Belle Creek.
Perilous place, I thought, to get lives started.
    All the bikers on the bike trail
might stop to have a look. Some curious kid
    might flip her over with a stick.
We walked the river trail talking easily again
    after twenty years. We spoke
of old friends, poets who died young:
    Ernesto Trejo, Charles Moulton, Larry Levis.
We are the caretakers, now, of their absence.
    Every spring from now on
the leaves will be saying Levis,
    and some will remember how once
he said, ". . . Filling with light,
    each leaf feels its way out,
Each a mad bible of patience."
    I hear his insomniac drumming
late at night above the swimming pool
    his grandfather dug with the help of mules.
I hear his voice finding new ways
    through the night.

All week beneath a canopy of leaves
    we've walked the Cannon River trail

alert for animals, matching birds
    to their names — indigo bunting,
rose-breasted grosbeak, American redstart, yellow warbler,
    adding them to our life lists.
At the big pond, we could count on
    the great blue heron to be there
perched on a snag, overseer of the water,
    or standing in the shallows
mirrored in stillness. Today the heron
    was gone and there was much splashing
and swirling in the pond. Something
    swam in circles in the weedy water
like otters at play. Flashes of bronze,
    waving leaves of dorsal fins and tails
told us they were carp. They seemed to be
    paired up, making such a big
commotion we guessed they were spawning.
    When we came to where the turtle
had buried her eggs, something
    had dug them up and feasted.
We counted twenty-nine empty eggs
    like torn-open ping-pong balls.
We passed between a doe and her fawn.
    Each moved off a few steps
into the green woods. The doe fixed us
    a moment in her wild gaze.
Another worried mother. All our lists
    are growing longer.

Juan Ramón Jiménez wrote, "I am not I.
    I am this one. . . . The one who
will remain standing when I die."
    When I die, someone will go on standing
by the lakes in your eyes, pressing your heart,
    kissing your breasts,
first one and then the other.
    The glorious love-making will continue,

and every drop of sweat
    will be a blessing on the earth.

Still I love to feel my own body
    around me. I love to feel your body
and your body feeling mine.
    And when our bodies are so close,
so into each other, we seem to be
    one animal, or one element
like water moving down a mountain.
    Or maybe we are going the other way,
up along the paths of nerve and skin,
    beginning to sweat and moan
when some fierce spirit picks us up,
    mashes us together
and shakes us until the trembling
    leaves our bodies
and we lie panting on the shore
    beside a clear stream or muddy lake
where our breaths and heartbeats
    hold their own a moment
among the leaves.

Two

Elegy for the Duke of Earl

PROLOGUE: MONSTROUS FAMILIES

"I spoke of [the Duke of Earl] and others
as well, but failed to realize that I had allowed
their names to function ambiguously. This proved
an embarrassment to me in that my oversight
has served to raise two pertinent objections.

It was argued that I had not properly
described [the Duke of Earl] or his work
and that my handling of [same] was pitifully
inadequate in terms of the totality of his thought.

It was argued that I had created *monstrous
families* by bringing together [the Duke of Earl]
and Linnaeus or in placing [the Duke of Earl]
next to Darwin in defiance of the most readily
observable family resemblances and natural ties."

"When we say [the Duke of Earl] we are using
a name that means one or a series—"

Duke Duke Duke Duke of Earl
Duke Duke Duke of Earl Duke Duke
Duke of Earl Duke Duke

1. THE FLYING RED HORSE

It was a nice old two story house
four or five of us rented
for seventy-five dollars a month.
The neighborhood was condemned
to make room for a new freeway.
We were a free-flowing family of transients,
soldiers back from the war, musicians,

students, dogs. We were known
for our parties. We took in strays.
We bought rice in fifty pound sacks,
beer by the case. We had a male
basset hound named Crash. And once
when our neighbor's poodle, across the street,
came into heat, we put Crash in an upstairs
bedroom, closed the door, but left the windows
open. A few of us were leaning on someone's car
in the street when Crash came out the window,
sniffed the air, whined, and began to pace
back and forth along the roof above the porch.
Before anyone could get to him,
he leapt from the roof.
I can still see him in the air
like the flying red horse above the Mobil
station, his deep chest, short legs, long ears
straight up, and the wild look in his eye.
He came down right on the points
of the picket fence, took out two boards,
gashed his belly, let out a howl,
stood up, shook himself, and headed across
the street, oblivious to his bleeding.
We all laughed. That was how we lived then.

2. WHATEVER HAPPENED TO J.C.?

I asked my brother, whatever happened to J.C.?
He said the last he heard J.C. was working
on a road crew somewhere down south.

Jesus Contreras, citizen of the United States,
friend, part Mexican part Mescalero Apache
part philosopher part coyote stood five-four

in his court shoes and weighed about as much
as your best bad dream, or a skin bag
full of peyote buttons. He left California

dragging his history behind him in the dust
like a broken chain. When my brother
introduced us, I saw the chain and shook his hand

that bore a blue tattoo of the cross
with blue lines suggesting radiance.
I hugged my brother who I hadn't seen in years

and welcomed them into the house.
We broke out beers and stories around the kitchen
table, and rode those horses late into night.

By dawn we were all brothers. We went out
into the desert to be part of the sunrise.
We picked the hard beans of jojoba

to sell to a dealer in town, who trucked them
to California to be rendered into essential oils
for cosmetics, soap, and shampoo.

We picked our way to a delicate delirium
under a blaring sun. We sang and danced
and roughed around in creosote, sat down

in ironwood and paloverde shade
to shelter with scorpions and tarantulas.
We did the snake, the owl, the wren.

We gave each other nicknames: I was Hunger,
my brother, Thirst. J.C., depending on the mood,
was Blood or Skin or Bait. Bait

for his uncanny knack of attracting
agents of the law, when all he wanted
was a little slack, all he needed was a little

respect, and one clear vision to free him
from his name, one clear vision
to give him his true name. Last time

I saw him he was standing at one of the old
crossroads with his thumb in the air
smiling, saying, see you on the news.

3. EVENING NEWS

He comes home from work, tired,
his mind braking and accelerating,
weaving through the day's traffic
of acts and images—the slim hooker
in yellow heels strolling the shoulder
of Biscayne Boulevard, Tina Turner's voice
sweating, the astronauts flaming out
like meteorites over the Atlantic,
a rusted shopping cart tipped over
a curb, its burden lifted, its ghost fled.

He puts the key in the door.
The small green lizard on the wall
above the mailbox cocks its head
and holds still as if listening.
I'm home, he says, and opens
the door, steps into the familiar room,
into the quietest moment of the day.

He turns on the news. He sips his beer.
They are showing a poorly focused,
unsteady video segment taken by a bystander

of a shirtless man stabbing another man
on a canal overpass in Miami Beach
just blocks away. Jesus, he says,
what am I supposed to do?
The news anchor says it began apparently
as an argument over money.
The men were friends. One
owed the other ten dollars.

He turns off the news. He runs the video
backwards in his mind. The shirtless man
rises from the railing, his friend
bursts up from the bloody water,
flips over the railing, lands on his feet,
grabs the bare shoulders of his friend,
who pulls the knife from his chest,
steps back quickly, swallowing his curses,
hiding the knife, moving back across
the line into a life of debt and anger,
friendship and choice, a life, now his,
he must invent the next move for.

He goes to the back window, stares
at the uncut grass. From somewhere
a bird, a painted bunting, alights
with a claim from the offices of air —
chartreuse, flame red, indigo blue.
The bird says, this is for you.

4. SONG: THE DAY THE DUKE OF EARL DIED

It was a day like spring in Babylon.
The mothers of the streets
were waiting for birth.
In the earth of their bodies
earth was busy.

The youths were confused,
their eyes seemed to run.
Funerals of the murdered
went on and on. More were murdered
and the sky yawned,
the day the Duke of Earl died.

The day the Duke of Earl died
was like a song one heard
at the end of a list—
said do this and this and this.
And this was a day like spring in Babylon.
The fathers of the streets
were waiting and waiting.
In the earth of their bodies
earth was busy
the day the Duke of Earl died.

When they looked in the coffin
and saw inside
everyone knew, but only a few cried.
It seemed like everyone
but no one was there,
including the Duke and the dogs of his hair
gone gray and wild
this day like spring in Babylon.

EPILOGUE: MORE OF THE SAME

   "Storytellers continued their narratives
late into the night to forestall death
and delay the inevitable moment
when everyone must fall silent."

   "[The Duke of Earl's] story is a desperate
inversion of murder; it is the effort,

throughout all those nights, to exclude death
from the circle. . ."

> *Duke Duke Duke Duke of Earl*
> *Duke Duke Duke of Earl Duke Duke*
> *Duke of Earl Duke Duke*

Amaryllis

Dark turns darker—a slight jolt of fear,
that chemical call and response
of gland and heart, opens my eyes.

Someone is standing over the bed?

Music not quite audible, the sense
of beat and sway.
           Amaryllis,
tall and leaning by the window in the dark.
Corollas, back to back cornets
blowing mute to the four corners
through falling snow.

Open petals around six blind stamens,
           sperm-laden anthers
around the long slightly curved pistil
splitting into three stigma.

Bless the senses and their echoes.

Music—a moth entering the flower—beat implied
the way an animal is implied by its tracks in snow.

Darkness, my eyes are open.
Black January, I'm listening.

Morphine

On the table as morphine dripped
in the IV, before he floated away
beyond care, he watched his body
below the heart lengthen

and distance itself across the room
where the masked surgeon worked
with knives and clips in green mist
of a rising tide. He never slept

but dreamed of good work, loading
and splitting, hauling, cradling,
lifting, pushing, sweating. Work
and love mixed together—fuel

and glue of our days. Then the walls
of muscles tearing, insides pushing out,
a little at first, then embarrassingly,
then frighteningly. Drifting above

the body, away from the body
being repaired, walls of the temple
being restored, except for one small
tributary cut and dammed for good,

thought of all the live sperm spilled
or trapped or given into another,
love and work mixed together.
Out there in the morphine

he felt sad and then nothing—
never slept, but when it wore off
and pain came to visit the incisions,
he wakened to it, almost grateful.

As Sparks Fly Upward

We built underground grottos, trenches
and passageways among cool rooms
of dirt. We placed boards, plywood
and papers over the trenches and rooms
and covered them with dirt, camouflaging
our work with trash and broken glass
to make it unattractive to walk on our roofs.
We left openings for ladders, openings
for light. We spoke in codes to set
ourselves apart. We studied crumbling walls,
the architecture of trees, theologies
of grass. We considered our bodies.
We constructed many-leveled fortresses
among the leaves, secreted away ammo
and forbidden texts. I am trying to remember
just what went on in those rooms
where we groped toward knowledge of good
and evil and tried out roles of hero,
servant, thief. We built up and tore
down, plotted and brooded, found
power and grace. And once
in the variegated light of a dream
warehouse we made of packing crates
stolen from orchards and vineyards
with labels of sunny peaches, clusters
of blue-black grapes, sharp-eyed swallows
winging over row crops, so many bright
pictures we had turned inward to catch
the light from between the slats, frescoes
in a crate cathedral, we watched a girl
take off her clothes and throw them
down the way an angel might cast off
shame. As sparks flew upward, our
cathedral burned with trouble like a home.

Blossom

Clovis, California

Blossom was fourteen, one of the wise and lovely.
She rode the palomino mare wild across the pasture,
her black hair streaming in the wind she made.
I watched her grow smaller as she headed hard

for the far barbed wire fence. At the last instant she cut
and leaned like a barrel racer, dirt splashing
from the hooves, then she straightened up the mare
and bore down on me where I stood still as a post,

stirred by her power. It would be years before
I made any sort of sense of those stirrings, and more
years before the wish, building there bareback
in the sun, murky as a drop of sweat that darkened

the faded denim, could come anywhere close to true.
But so what if I couldn't hang on at full gallop
and would slide farther and farther back as she
urged the big horse to pound the field faster

until I felt each hoof-surge in my skinny thighs
and clung fiercely to the tail of the mare,
bouncing like a stuffed monkey tied to a bumper.
And so what if a rear hoof caught my kneecap

and split it down the middle as I fell, first
on my coccyx and then on my face in the hard
clods of the San Joaquin. And so what if the years
have painted with primaries and filed away the pain

and embarrassment and trashed the context.
Just as true ideas may arise among the ignorant

and humble, when she smiled down on me,
muddy sweat dripping from her chin, her breasts

rising and falling, her heart visibly pounding,
and offered me her strong hand, I aspired
to mount the mare and ride with Blossom wherever.

Red Sweatshirt with Embroidered Wave

Redondo Beach, California

Five of them, two standing, and three sitting
on the edge of the cliff, breathless,
where the jade-green ice plant spills down

to the sand, all wearing red sweatshirts,
all looking out at the horizon
beyond the Palos Verdes peninsula

where the hazy morning sky is turning
from deep gray to blue, and the water
in the bay is beginning to light up

with tones of green, blue, and an elusive
soft yellow broken by glints of mica
riding the big swells coming in

from the far west, lifting, sweeping, pounding
the inner chambers of these attentive hearts
who wear the sign of the wave

embroidered on their shirts, and look on
rapt, eager to be intimate
with such power, yet wary. They are trying

to decide. Should they go out at Topaz
or Sapphire Street? Or should they stay here
where they are safe, no one says, and just watch.

Now a sixth, wearing the same red shirt
walks toward them along Camino Real.
Now they are all standing, taking off their shirts.

Fireworks

The sidewalks are cracked and buckled
with drop-offs and swells. That's how
I like them. It makes the walk better.
Heaved up by ice and roots, waves
of the seasons moving along the streets,
a kind of stream if we could speed up
the film or see like trees.
I have to keep looking down, and that means
I have to keep looking up. "Levanta
la cabeza!" they shouted from the bar
in Ensenada at the one dancing fiercely
alone in his fifteenth year. What
have I learned? That the next line
may take months, and the right words
have to overcome and overcome
to return to the clear waters of their birth.
That when one is mired in a tar pit
another is lighting a match. That Fourth
of July, drunk, the two of us couldn't do
the simplest thing. I held the cherry bomb.
He lit the match. I must have been
looking up at a burst of fireworks
over the South Bay, and that threw
the timing off, so that when I looked
down my hand burst, orange, and blue sparks
shot up my arm into my skull. They
are still there. Looking down deeper,
it is this other quieter explosion I see.
The one who danced alone in Ensenada,
older now, sits in the sun on a hot rock
with his feet in the cold stream. He looks up
as she eases herself down. Aspen leaves
tremble and water pulls the sunlight
in glittering strands over the rocks.

On the Road

Nayarit, Mexico

When the soldier with the machine gun
shot the iguana out of the false banyan tree
it wasn't a movie, just a kid showing off.
When the bloody iguana fell from the limb
twitching in the air and landed with a wet
thud, he smiled or grinned as lizards do.
Cautious but unafraid, I wore the same
armor of youth and could see the limit
in his face. The birds were silent
for less than a minute. Cars drove by
as usual like ants in their diligence.

Indian River

Miami Beach, Florida

Though it may not be *Indian* or *river*
I love the words and what they stand for.

As a child, I sat on the concrete banks
and fished for fish while white cabin cruisers

and gray workaday diesel launches made waves
in the water in the mind my fishing line

cut through. The line held still while everything
around it moved — pastel Cadillacs flashing

on the causeway, black vultures circling on thermals
above city hall, barracuda chasing snapper

in a fan of light that closed. Brain coral
lay in the water, in the wash of the surf

thinking slowly. The great pink hotel Barcelona
shouldered the sky and aimed hundreds of windows

at the Atlantic. It too a kind of coral thinking.
What to make of the world destroyed? What

to make of what was coming? Tan,
don't burn the white hemispheres.

Don't wake me from this sub-tropical dream
of continuous Sundays where *Indian*

names the water like a blessing
and *river* is river all the way to the sea.

Lamp Without a Shade

Lagunitas, California

If you followed this beam of light
down through dripping pines you'd come
to an old rotting house with broken windows
where a young man hears the soulful notes,
like smoke in the rain, but can't make them
come out of the flute. It's January, a rainy month
along the coast range, the night the postal worker,
the young man's neighbor with seven kids,
will park his car at the end of the road, run
a hose from the tailpipe through the wind wing
and fix it in place with a clump of rag.
The young man hears the music, but it's no use.
He's been trying for hours. If he didn't have
to play so softly he might be able to do it.
If he could blow the sax, but the sax is gone,
and his one good pair of shoes, his class ring,
and all the books and records he kept in a peach crate
beside his makeshift bed, a mattress on a door
on cinder blocks. All that's left are the clothes
he's wearing, the clothes in his pack,
the jungle boots, the flute, half a pack of cigarettes,
and the lamp without a shade plugged in
to an orange extension cord which runs
along the wet ground to the house next door,
house of the kind couple and their seven kids,
who agreed to this arrangement so the young man
would have a place to crash, as we used to say,
and a light to read by. He hears the notes,
feels them move his body. He rocks, sways,
taps his foot, but the flute's metal breaks
his breath. He lights a cigarette.
Such a small defeat, the scale won't balance.
He breaks down the flute, cleans the three parts

inside and out with a small rag and a rod,
lays the silver pieces in their blue velvet slots,
closes the case, turns out the lamp, and feels
a sudden rush of cold damp air and can't decide
if the clouds inhaled or the whole dark house
just opened to receive the rain.

Green

We drove south along the Mora River
on the narrow road with no shoulder.
Grass and wildflowers grew right up
to the edge of the asphalt. The cattle
were fat and standing in grass so green

and tall you couldn't see their legs.
The cottonwoods arched over the road
in places and their leaves clattered,
leaves like small mittened hands,
pale green on one side, paler green

on the other, flicking back and forth
in the breeze with a sound like riffles
in the river. It looked more like Virginia
than New Mexico, until you got a few
hundred yards from the river and the land

spread out toward the east and drifted away
on the Llano Estacado. Even the wind
was green. *Verde viento. Verdes ramas.*
As Lorca said. We were dreaming
of the big rainbows in the lake

and the steaming pot of beans, tortillas
and salsa Forminia was preparing
in the ranch house at the end of the road.
After lunch on our way to the lake,
where we planned to wade out

chest deep, tie on black marabou streamers
and send them out on long casts
into storied water, we stopped to say

hello to Chope, the old cowboy
who has tended this land forty years,

and give him the jar of honey
we brought for him from Chimayo.
He said he hadn't seen the land this green
in all the years he'd lived here.
"Take a good look, boys," he said,
"you won't see it this green again."

Unfinished Story

Like a quilt made from scraps, torn pieces of old dresses,
the yokes of shirts long out of fashion, curtains untouched
by the sun for decades that seem, still, to hold the tinny
music that once blew through them, I am trying to put
together the story my mother never finished telling me.

I knew my uncle Laurence as a kind man who drank
and smiled and drank and went away. When he ended up
in Bellevue with delirium tremens, after he began
to recover, according to my mother, because he was such
a big help with the other patients, the doctors didn't want
to let him out. He should have been a nurse, she said.

She was not yet born, though she might have heard the blast,
and probably felt the surge of adrenalin and the fear
that shook her mother, Ada, as she ran awkwardly, late
in her eighth month, toward the house and into the room
where her three little girls had been napping.

I wonder if the movie may have nuanced the afternoon—
the way the young are eager to act out what they see
on the screen, the squint-eyed hero taking aim on
the villain. I wonder what movie it was making the rounds
of the coal camps and hill towns of eastern Kentucky
in that long-gone late spring.

Her father, Jim, had taken the boys, Laurence and Ralph,
to town to see the movie, maybe their first one ever.
As boys do, on the way home they ran ahead of their
father. It was late April or early May, six weeks before
she was born. I imagine the apple trees in bloom.

The big willow where the boys had carved their initials,
L.T.P., Laurence Theodore Peters, and R.C.P., Ralph
Commodore Peters, would have been bright green in
full leaf. When my mother told the story it was always
in fragments, always arising from some other context.
If she shied away from some crucial point, it would have

been cruel to press her. After all, the story, a pall in the house
she was born into, came to her in just such fragments,
withholdings and turnings away. The stark details remain:
Papa had loaned his shotgun to a neighbor, I hear her say.
When the neighbor came to return the gun no one
was home, so he slipped it through the open kitchen window
onto the table. When the boys came in, one of them
picked up the gun. Laurence said they knew it wasn't loaded
because they had seen Papa fire the last shell at a hawk.

They went to the bedroom where their three little sisters,
Ruby, Ruth, and Jewel, were napping or playing in the bed.
The boys sat at the foot of the bed passing the gun back
and forth, showing off, talking about the movie. Laurence
aimed the shotgun at Ralph's face and pulled the trigger.
The walls, the girls, the bed were bathed in the boy's blood
and pieces someone would have had to clean up.

Ada came running. Jim came running.

I look and look and can't see Laurence.

Years later when Laurence would disappear, not show up
for dinner, my mother said, Papa would send me out
to bring him back from the big tree where he sat and sang
"oh bury me beside my brother beneath the willow tree."

Mama was in shock over Ralph's death and never cared
much for me, my mother said, and changed the subject
to the time she met Albert Einstein aboard a ship docked

in Miami. She was holding me in her arms, and, according to my mother, Einstein patted my head and said, "What a beautiful baby."

Three

We Are

Nogales, Sonora

Maybe we are not supposed to be here
but we are. We bump our hips together

as we walk. The town is lit with brilliant
mid-morning winter sun, the sky a soft

accepting blue. Old cars and battered trucks
move slowly up and down the streets.

A blaze of sun on chrome or glass, half
a line of impassioned song, a woman's voice,

stone grin of a man with a tower of caged
songbirds — we are swept and swayed.

A raven croaks twice from the top of a sign
shaped as a boot. Gold tassels bounce

in the windows of a bus. Young men stare
in envy and lust. With each step the street

is more and more ours until it seems we are
the business it goes on about. I pick up

a tin fish with hammered scales but have
to set it back down quickly so my hand

can return to the small of her back.
An old woman in a bright red rebozo

calls us her dear ones, as if the desire aglow
in our bodies were already making a family.

Zahkia

Highway City, California

Once a week Zahkia Famie made the trip
to the butcher to ask after the legs of lamb.
After inspecting what lay chilled in the case
and what the butcher lifted from its hook
in the cold box, after careful deliberations
based on several lifetimes of experience
in the markets of the Middle East
and the peculiar culinary esthetic handed down
through the family for generations, after
commenting on the weather and inquiring
about the health of the butcher, his wife,
his children, she made her selection
and paid with cash. Though her tongue
was at times as sharp as her knives,
she sang behind the screens of her kitchen
or beneath the olive trees as she cut
the lamb into portions and set aside the fat
for soap. What she thought about the Doors,
"Purple Haze," and the young men and women
who swam naked in her water trough,
only a native speaker of Arabic could say.
Matriarch of the secret gardens
on the outskirts of Highway City, where
illegal soldiers of fortune slept beneath
the poisonous oleanders and whole families
came with buckets to harvest the fallen figs,
she dispensed wisdom like a turtle, grace
like a fox, and fed whoever was hungry.
I don't know if her gift was dignity or craft,
though she possessed both in abundance.
What I took from her was what I needed
most, a temporary home and that kind
of confidence the uprooted young take

from the steadfast old. She didn't seem
to notice the screaming in the orchard.
She didn't stare at the full moon
from the bottom of the water trough.
She didn't scrape the black powder
from the bullet to light the hookah
with a flash. She rose each day
at dawn and watered the tomatoes.

The Hog Boss

It must have been a hot day, the air still, sun pushing down
on the big aluminum barn, when the hog boss and his nephew
entered the cloying shade to clean out the pits. One doesn't get
used to the stink. Better to say they were prepared for it,

the way any workers are prepared to reenter the atmosphere
in which they work, once they've worked awhile. The boss
especially. The boss is supposed to know. The fish boss knows
the fish, the road boss knows the road, the fire boss . . . and so on.

But the nephew, when he went down, was not prepared
for the overwhelming fumes, gases of decomposing manure
pooled and etherizing in the pit. The boy began to work,
listening without thought to ruminations of the hogs,

the whole barn an engine, a ticking and liquid rumbling
like a diesel idling, an engine of the afternoon of which
he was a part. He remembered his uncle standing above him
on the metal grates, pacing a little, talking. Then the voice

fading away, body and soul swimming off in different
directions. Later they said the hog boss went down
and hoisted up the boy onto the grates where there
was some air. He must have heard the shovel stop

in the muck and wondered at the long stillness that followed.
He must have called into the pit, and when there was
no answer lowered himself down. He must have been
puzzled at what he found. He lifted the boy out of the pit

as the fumes began to stir his brain and squeeze his heart.
Did he hear hooves on the grates, shit falling like hail

on the crops? Did he call once to the boy, his wife,
his mother? Did he curse the gas or pray to the Lamb?

Did he fail into the engine or fall away from the earth?
Later his wife said, "His thirty-two years of very hard work
were done. We can't put a question mark when the Lord
had put a period." Propped by the door of the barn, shading

his eyes from the sun, the nephew watched as three
men carried his uncle out into the yard, pumped
the chest, and blew their own breaths into his mouth.
He didn't think about it then, as he watched first

one man and then another bow down and place
his lips to the lips of his uncle, how now he
would be the hog boss, and all of his working days
he would remember only part of how it came to pass.

Small Pleasures

Mojave Desert, California

Noon, one hundred fourteen degrees, no breeze
except the breeze we make
going ten miles an hour in the pickup,
no road, just open flat desert, low brush
and scattered rock, the Mojave
somewhere west of Edwards Air Force Base.
We're eating our sandwiches, the boss and I,
drinking cups of cold water from the thermos jug
on the seat between us. We carry
three gallons of water for each man
to get us through to four o'clock,
when we head for cold beer at the bar.
He hasn't said anything for some time,
just chews and drinks, chews and drinks,
stares out at the heat waves
as the pickup bumps along. Covered with dust
and oil, we've been out here since five a.m.
working on the road. Now we're leaving
the road behind. Last night, stopped
at a phone booth on the way to the motel,
I watched moths swarm at the light
while he tried to call home, was it?
Something was wrong, bad connection, something.
He got angry, yanked the phone off the cord
and threw it on the ground. He didn't try
to explain, and I didn't ask.
We went to our rooms and slept.
We've finished our lunch and cigarettes.
I look over thinking to say something
about how a day like this makes me appreciate
small pleasures, a little shade, this cushioned
seat, a cold tomato with salt, but his
fifty-year-old eyes are closed, his head

fallen to one side, mouth open, hands
in his lap, no longer steering.
Out here it doesn't seem to matter.
Even the snakes, tortoises, and horned lizards
are underground. It's a big desert
and we're all alone. I lean back,
close my eyes. This too
is a pleasure, moving off into the open
where the work is never done.

Derailed Train

New Orleans, Louisiana

The train, with its sleepers breathing away
shifts in dream mills, window gazers
studying lights like glyphs on cave walls,
a young couple, and others lulling over drinks
and papers, talking night-talk in low tones,

the train locks its brakes in a long screech
and sprawl of sparks, rocks, jolts, slams
to a stop in the dark. Adrenalin surges
like radiant heat, pounds in the muscles
of hearts—what happened, what happened.

What is this memory good for? What does it mean
to hold this scene that keeps its freshness
twenty years or more, though seldom recalled,
and feels, when remembered in detail, like
an awakening still going on—light

of a dead star pulsing and flickering
in space, shining in place on the surface
of moving water. Lights in the train
come on again, and they are fixed a moment,
prisoners in a strip-search, naked in the glare

of their fear. They turn away from each other
as if to dress, like adulterers readying
to resume known lives made strange.
I think it was the built-up force
of their withholding that did this.

I think if I get off the train a few hours
later and follow this young couple I was once

a part of out of the station down Loyola
to Canal Street and into the French Quarter,
I will listen harder this time to hear

what they say. I am listening now.
Their heads are close together, they are speaking,
but a siren intrudes to block out their words,
a wailing that turns a corner and flashes away
under a disinterested moon floating above

the iron balconies. I follow them into Felix's
Oyster House and stand at the bar across
from their table and look at their young faces
nodding like two poppies in a breeze
that seem now to have nothing to say.

Their mouths are full of oysters. I turn away
and watch scarred black hands with a knife
flying among the oysters. Looking up,
through the smoky knots and loops
and loose braids of a jazz clarinet

weaving among the shuck and jive, I see
a face with plenty to say, but not to me.
I have to go now and walk with them
down Bourbon Street before I can climb
the stairs of delight in the Hotel Lafayette

and lie in the cool sheets beneath
the slowly turning blades of the ceiling fan
and stretch out and drift off with the sax
and the bass pulsing the cloth covered
wall speakers adorned with twin

treble clefs above the bed. Listen.
They are speaking again. She points

to an open door throbbing red
then blue to a bump-and-grind beat
where three nude dancers strut and

simulate to the slap and splash of a cymbal.
I lean closer, try to hear what they say,
but a hustling street barker drowns them out—
"We got boys, we got girls,
we got everything you want right here."

Back before hospitals, before grief, before
face-offs with invisible beasts,
before they lost each other I lost them
in the crowd among the amused,
the oblivious, the bereft.

If I back up just a little to that high
bridge above the Mississippi where the train
derailed, I can hear what they have to say.
I see them in the soft night air standing
in the opening between coupled cars

with another passenger, a man on his way
home from Houston. As if on
one of *the great monsters lying low,*
they are all looking down at the lights
of the city and the tugs and barges

moving slowly on the river.
"Just beautiful," one of them says.

The Rose

Fix an orgasm so it stays?

I don't know. It would probably kill you.

How do you represent one to a world dying for one,
a world that won't admit such a thing exists?

You build a frame, a strong frame. You get some plaster, some rags.
You imagine a rose opening that goes on opening,
but the petals don't fall, the petals disappear, leaving strong
bright lines radiating through layers and layers of time
outward from and inward to a definite center.

Jay De Feo wanted to make something that "had a center to it."
She worked on it every day in her apartment for eight years.

It was eleven feet high and weighed 2,300 lbs.
when she was evicted and had to stop her work.

They had to get a crane and a crew of strong men
to remove it from the upstairs apartment.
Bruce Conner made a movie of the event, and in it
Jay De Feo looks sad. *Up you go little smoke.*
Dear Landlord, Go to Hell.

Where is the brave and beautiful Jay De Feo now?
They say the paint she worked with killed her. I don't know.

Jay De Feo made *Doctor Jazz, Applaud the Black Fact, Deathwish,*
and then she made *The Rose.*

◡

What is the right music for this?

Slow blues, smoky jazz, mourning dove in dusk?

Dust and dirt will do, will do as they have always done —
hold us up, cover us, muddy the water, soften the light.

Through the dust I see a sunflower and a woman walking away.
Light steps in fine dirt, raked and smoothed, soft

to cushion the fall of figs in the orchard, gone orchard
of the San Joaquin.

Naked in late afternoon light, barefoot on the soft dirt,
down a row of fig trees loaded with fruit about to fall,
she walks — no way to describe those steps without stumbling.

She walks and then she runs, gone in her pleasure, her pain,
gone down a long converging row of silvery contorted bodies
in the last orchard, and each step raises a small cloud
of golden dust I lean into trying to coax another transubstantiation,

dust into water, pallor into blush, a closed unimagined space
into the rose.

American Flamingo

I know he shot them to know them.
I did not know the eyes of the flamingo
are blue, a deep live blue.

And the tongue is lined with many small
tongues, thirteen, in the sketch
by Audubon, to function as a sieve.

I knew the long rose-pink neck,
the heavy tricolored down-sweeping bill,
the black primaries.

But I did not know the blue eye
drawn so passionately by Audubon
it seems to look out, wary, intense,

from the paper it is printed on.
                                        —what
Is man but his passion?

asked Robert Penn Warren. In the background
of this sketch, tenderly subtitled *Old Male*,
beneath the over-draping feathered

monument of the body, between the long
flexible neck and the long bony legs
covered with pink platelets of flesh,

Audubon has given us eight postures,
eight stunning movements in the ongoing
dance of the flamingos.

Once at Hialeah in late afternoon,
I watched the satin figures of the jockeys
perched like bright beetles on the backs

of horses pounding down the home
stretch, a few crops whipping
the lathering flanks, the loud flat

metallic voice of the announcer fading
as the flamingos, grazing the pond water
at the far end of the infield rose

in a feathery blush, only a few feet
off the ground and flew one long
clipped-winged ritual lap

in the heavy Miami light, a great
slow swirl of grace from the old world
that made tickets fall from hands,

stilled horses, and drew toasts from the stands
as they settled down again
like a rose-colored fog on the pond.

Blues on the 4th of July

Portland, Oregon

Black back of the submarine moored
    across the river
absorbs the late sun.
    Lone shirtless rockers
and swaying couples keep the beat,
    dance in place
in the growing crowd. Bluesman, Shorty,
    pulls his fretted electric guitar
between his legs, jumps down
    from the stage.
Holding the hips of his ax
    he moves out into the parting crowd,
head bobbing over the steel strings,
    playing cries and shrieks
with his tongue and teeth.
    People line up along the bridge
above the river—small black silhouettes
    gathering for the fireworks.
Standing up there in the high twilight
    looking down,
they could be the spirits of the ones
    who died young, the ones who fucked
like fiends, smoked marijuana, hash,
    and opium at the opening
of the war. The ones who danced
    on the San Francisco docks—
James Cotton and his band on a flatbed
    rail car in the sun
wailing blues in waves over the hairy
    shirtless acid trippers
getting psyched, as we said, for whatever
    independence might have in store.

The harp howls, the drum
        rocks the living, the dead drift off
in the dark, and the bluesman sings
        a Big Joe Turner tune:

        Mama won't ya jump me
        in your Hollywood bed
        Rock me pretty mama
        til my face turns cherry red

Whose eye stares from the top
        of this pyramid
the music sets adrift above the city?
        Does it matter? the blues asks.
I'll put a little salt water in it.
        I'll make it shine.

Kindness of Strangers

Nevada, 1965

He washed down Mexican dexadrine
with Old Crow and Old Crow with beer.
His dark blue Mercury shook at eighty
like his hand.

I kept him in the corner of my left eye,
wondering what catastrophe he was leaving
behind and racing toward.

I didn't say a word.

After he watched me eat at a crossroads diner,
he handed me a trembling ten
and was gone into heat waves
on the road aimed east.

Just over the horizon under the desert's skin
they were making a new inferno,
off limits even to the damned.

Look at the stars. You can almost touch them.
The years stumble and bow before such space.

Orion's shaft, Cassiopeia between Cepheus
and Andromeda, famous galactic families,

dogs and horses of the heavens, cool
glittering distant millions

on a black velvet dome over the desert
just off highway 50 west of Ely

under a single Joshua tree
leaning a little toward the east,

she slips out of her blue jeans,
accomplice of visions and pleasures

on the road over basin and range.
We gaze at stars until we too

stumble and bow, and the radio tuned to Salt Lake
drifts in and out of songs all night.

⌣

Saturday night downtown Wendover.
The Badgers or the Hornets have just
beat the hell out of the Yellowjackets
or the Panthers. The empire
of the main drag is once again
under the rule of hormones and beer.

Have no fear, I tell myself, no fear.
The only stoplight for hundreds of miles
keeps opening and closing its red eye,
and even the shards of glass at my feet
pulse like pieces of a heart. I'm packing
a pocketknife, *Leaves of Grass* in paperback,
and two bloodshot eyes I intend to feast
on New York's neon apples.

Give me a lift or leave me alone.

The moon is bad, the spoon is bent,
the dish is empty, the cow can't jump,
the same white Impala going up and down
the main in a haze of hard rock,
same Chevrolet that let go a fusillade

of bottles last time around stops
and offers me a ride to the outskirts of town.

Taillights fade and the road goes quiet.
Stars over the power lines hum.

Little red rooster crows awhile
then falls back into stupor.

Let the sun rise
and stretch its rays over the salt flats
of Utah and touch the sleeping body
in the mosquito bog at the side of the road,
the one who doesn't want to waken yet
from his dream of the kindness of strangers.

Keet Seel

Diné Bike'yah, Arizona

We set out to soak in some eternity,
to be held by the canyon in the canyon
as the Anasazi were, to feel
sun-warmth coming out of sandstone,
to feel that respiration, give and take,
wind and wave that made the dune
that holds still in the cliff.

We set out to walk into the maze,
befriended, and meet it half way —
the whole place coming, as it is,
to reside in us.

We drove up through Leupp
past the Kachina Cliffs to Kykotsmovi,
then up 264 to Moenkopi and Tuba City,
then up 160 past Tonalea and Cow Springs.

Little juniper trees shimmied in wind
and red mud ran in rivulets
on all sides when we arrived on the rim
of Tsegi Canyon in a thunderstorm.

We sat in the truck and watched the rain
streaming over the windshield in torrents
and felt the percussive strikes of lightning,
the flash and boom close along the rim.
Air charged with ozone shown blue,
a light I remembered seeing underwater
once, blown from my board in storm surf
off the breakwater in Redondo, a watery blue
last light, maybe.

Then suddenly
as it came, thunder rumbled off to the east,
the wind slowed and rain fell lighter
and lighter and was swept away
by the departing storm.

We stepped out into air scented, it seemed,
with gratefulness. Pinyons and junipers glittered
with sunlight reflecting off myriad beads
of rain, the light forming in radiant circles
among the black branches. Out on the slickrock,
fresh reflecting pools mirrored flotillas of cumulus
crossing slowly the big blue. If rain is a festival,
as Thomas Merton said, the aftermath
of that storm on the rim of Tsegi Canyon,
the last hour of the day, was a pageant
of linked primordial parades—tortoises,
tarantulas, conga lines of ants. Flickers,
wrens, mountain bluebirds, and a platoon
of pinyon jays working through darkening junipers
as Jake and I lit a fire and watched
the sun slip away and stars come on.

↙

The next day we are walking up the canyon
and Jake is telling me about the last time
he had hiked to Keet Seel,
years ago, and how he had crossed
the shallow water of Laguna Creek
again and again, just as we are doing
now, walking in red sand
looking out for pools of quicksand,
feeling the sun on the sides of our faces,
heat radiating from the sandstone walls,
strong light flashing and sparking off

the water, and rounding a bend
to see a head-high stand
of magenta bee balm, and going
into it out of the quiet—a half acre
of flowers and bees idling like an engine.
Just as Jake recalls the pleasure
and peace of standing among the flowers
and feeling the energy of the bees,
we round a bend and there it is,
as if his memory has set the place before us.

Notes

"Elegy for the Duke of Earl" was written for more than one voice. All but the last three lines of the prologue and the epilogue are altered excerpts from Donald F. Bouchard and Sherry Simon's translation of "What Is an Author?" by Michel Foucault. "The Duke of Earl" is the title of a song by Gene Chandler popular in 1962.

"The Hog Boss" was suggested by, and quotes from, Laura Wilson's background notes to Richard Avedon's book of photographic portraits *In the American West.*

"Derailed Train," lines 49 and 50, were suggested by the following: "But why do you return to wretchedness? Why not climb up the mountain of delight, the origin and cause of every joy?" Canto I of *Inferno* by Dante Alighieri, translated by Allen Mandelbaum. Line 78, "the great monsters lying low," is from section 31 of *Song of Myself* by Walt Whitman.

Other Books in the Crab Orchard Series in Poetry

Muse
Susan Aizenberg

This Country of Mothers
Julianna Baggott

White Summer
Joelle Biele

In Search of the Great Dead
Richard Cecil

Twenty First Century Blues
Richard Cecil

Circle
Victoria Chang

Consolation Miracle
Chad Davidson

Names above Houses
Oliver de la Paz

The Star-Spangled Banner
Denise Duhamel

Beautiful Trouble
Amy Fleury

Pelican Tracks
Elton Glaser

Winter Amnesties
Elton Glaser

Fabulae
Joy Katz

Train to Agra
Vandana Khanna